Skilled Jobs in

WELLNESS AND BEAUTY

W.L. Kitts

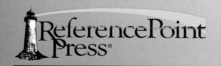

ReferencePoint Press®

San Diego, CA

About the Author

W.L. Kitts is a professional freelance writer and children's book author who lives in San Diego, California.

For more information, contact:
ReferencePoint Press, Inc.
PO Box 27779
San Diego, CA 92198
www.ReferencePointPress.com

Picture Credits:

Cover: Denys Kurbatov/Shutterstock.com
10: Simone Hogan/Shutterstock.com
19: Dragon Images/Shutterstock.com
32: Sergei Mironenko/Shutterstock.com
65: Prostock-Studio/Shutterstock.com

LIBRARY OF CONGRESS CATALOGING-IN-PUBLICATION DATA

Names: Kitts, W. L., author.
Title: Skilled jobs in wellness and beauty / by W.L. Kitts.
Description: San Diego, CA : ReferencePoint Press, 2020. | Series: Jobs for
  skilled workers | Includes bibliographical references and index.
Identifiers: LCCN 2019049374 (print) | LCCN 2019049375 (ebook) | ISBN
  9781682828274 (library binding) | ISBN 9781682828281 (ebook)
Subjects: LCSH: Health--Vocational guidance. | Beauty, Personal--Vocational
  guidance.
Classification: LCC RA777 .K58 1994 (print) | LCC RA777 (ebook) | DDC
  646.7/2023--dc23
LC record available at https://lccn.loc.gov/2019049374
LC ebook record available at https://lccn.loc.gov/2019049375

Contents

A Growing Industry

According to the Global Wellness Institute (GWI), the wellness and beauty field is a growing industry. In October 2018 the GWI stated that the industry—which includes fitness, alternative medicine, workplace wellness, spas, beauty, and nutrition—was a $4.2 trillion market. In addition, this market had grown by over 6 percent each of the previous two years.

Katherine Johnston, senior research fellow at the GWI, attributes the continued growth to the nation's increasing awareness that it is important to relax and care for oneself. Johnston says:

> Once upon a time, our contact with wellness was occasional: we went to the gym or got a massage. But this is changing fast: a wellness mindset is starting to permeate the global consumer consciousness. . . . Wellness, for more people, is evolving from rarely to daily, from episodic to essential, from a luxury to a dominant lifestyle value. And that profound shift is driving powerful growth.[1]

Individuals are not the only ones making wellness a priority—the corporate world is as well. Employees are working longer and harder. They are often always "on" because of smartphones that allow them to answer emails or return calls long after they leave their office. Companies realize the importance of having wellness programs to promote the physical, emotional, and mental well-being of their employees.

Adding to the trend is the fact that many services or practices that were once considered alternative, like meditation or massage, are now mainstream. As a result, a variety of new treatments has emerged. One such treatment is cryotherapy, which involves being enclosed in a chamber at -200°F (-129°C). This technique has been used to treat conditions ranging from back pain to weight loss to multiple sclerosis.

Another new technique known as forest bathing has clients immerse themselves in nature to help them sleep, fight depression, and boost their immune systems. Even traditional fitness classes are getting a makeover. From circus-inspired aerial workouts to naked fitness classes to Date-ercise—a circuit-type workout that matches men and women, similar to speed dating—fitness has become about much more than running on a treadmill.

There has also been an increase in wellness and beauty retreats, or wellness tourism. A mountain hike has been reimagined to incorporate meditation and yoga. A spa experience might feature a dip in an arctic bath, where one alternates between bathing in 39°F (4°C) ice water and then enclosing oneself in a heated sauna. To provide these rich and varied experiences, wellness centers increasingly offer multiple wellness and beauty options under one roof. For example, a popular New York athletic wear store offers fitness classes alongside spa and beauty services.

Something for Everyone

The emergence of these various experiences means there are a wide range of jobs in the wellness and beauty space. People who like hands-on healing might consider a career in Reiki or massage. For those who want to work with scents, a career in aromatherapy is a good choice. Someone who is kinesthetically oriented might want to explore being a personal trainer or a Zumba instructor. And creative types might have a calling as a makeup artist or hairstylist.

Another exciting change in the industry is that it is becoming open to more men. In the past male service providers (such as an esthetician or massage therapist) have found it challenging to obtain work. This is because the industry's mostly female client base is not always comfortable with men providing treatments such as bikini waxing. Conversely, female estheticians sometimes turn down male clients who seek similar intimate treatments. Julio Mendez, Chicago's first male esthetician, faced discrimination when first breaking into his field. Mendez explains, "When

I graduated I was told that women wouldn't allow me to work on them because I was a man."[2] But that did not stop Mendez, who was often the only male in the room during his training. In 2013 he opened his own salon. "I began noticing that there was a trend in men demanding professional spa and salon services,"[3] he says. Wax Man Spa provides full body waxing and hair trimming services for men, as well as other traditional spa treatments like facials. Mendez, who describes his clientele as those who want "a barber shop feel but with a salon spa service,"[4] has seen his business steadily grow.

A Rewarding Career

For students looking to follow this career path, there is more good news about the wellness and beauty industry: a majority of jobs within it require less than two years of postsecondary education. This means that those who are passionate about this field can spend less time in school and more time out in the field doing what they love and working directly with the public.

Esthetician

What Does an Esthetician Do?

Estheticians (also spelled aestheticians) are skin care specialists. They perform a wide range of facial and body treatments to enhance the health and look of a person's skin.

There are many different types of estheticians. Those who work in salons or spas offer treatments primarily intended to promote beauty or offer relaxation. Services include facials, chemical peels, hair removal, airbrush tanning, makeup application, eyelash extensions, and head and neck massage. Although estheticians do not diagnose or treat skin disorders, they may assess the condition of a client's skin and offer suggestions for care regimens and specific products.

Medical estheticians, on the other hand, work in clinical settings for dermatologists or reconstructive or cosmetic surgeons or are otherwise under the supervision of a licensed medical professional. In addition to performing regular esthetician duties, they work on patients who have skin problems like acne or psoriasis. Medical estheticians also provide pre-op and post-op care for cosmetic surgery clients, assisting with treatments to care for wounds or reduce scarring, for example. Some might teach burn victims how to apply makeup to cover scars or skin discolorations. Medical estheticians may also support medical professionals by taking clients' medical histories or vital signs.

Oncology estheticians, who work with clients who have cancer, modify spa treatments to this group's specific needs. For example, cancer patients often have sensitive skin as a result of their treatments and need a more gentle touch. Oncology estheticians might use massage to help them with nausea or insomnia. They may also use healing techniques such as reflexology, aromatherapy, and Reiki (a form of energy healing in which a practitioner places his or her hands on or just above the client's body). Other services might include tattooing the areolas to disguise breast cancer scars, teaching clients how to apply makeup to compensate for eyebrows that may have fallen out from chemotherapy, and fitting clients for wigs and prosthetics.

Becky Kuehn is a medical esthetician who owns Oncology Spa Solutions. Her work was sparked by her own journey with cancer. "I remembered the women I encountered in my own cancer experience and I wanted to do more, give back," she says. So she began volunteering with the American Cancer Society's Look Good Feel Better program and was immediately struck by the courage and strength of the women she met. "I wanted to do more," she explains. "So, I approached an oncology center and asked if I could have a treatment room and perform skin care treatments on their cancer patients."[5]

Regardless of which path an esthetician chooses, most love what they do and find it rewarding to help people look and feel better about themselves. Celebrity esthetician Renée Rouleau, who works with clients such as Demi Lovato, practically grew up in a salon. Her grandmother was a hairstylist with her own business. Rouleau explains, "I always just loved watching her and how she was helping people look beautiful and feel beautiful and that resonated with me my whole life and so when I was choosing my career path, I followed in her footsteps; . . . 23 years later I just love what I do."[6]

A Typical Workday for a Salon Esthetician

A typical day for salon or spa estheticians depends on what treatments they are going to perform. They might have five or six clients, depending on the length of each treatment booked. They might do a facial for one client, followed by a massage or a body wrap for the next. Another client might book a waxing appointment, and yet another might book an airbrush tanning or eyelash extensions. In between clients, estheticians need to clean their work space. They must sanitize their equipment and replace any sheets or towels used by the previous client.

In addition to seeing clients, estheticians usually have to order products and supplies. If they are self-employed, estheticians most likely answer phones, return calls, and book appointments when not with clients. They may have to handle customer payments as well as do light bookkeeping duties and banking. Estheticians who own a spa or salon would also be responsible for hiring, scheduling, and training staff. And whether they own the

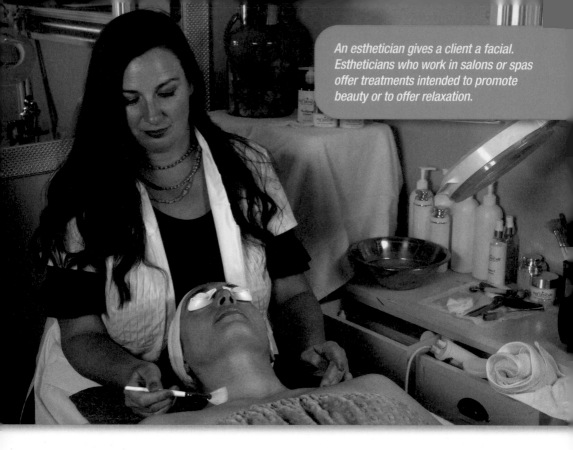

An esthetician gives a client a facial. Estheticians who work in salons or spas offer treatments intended to promote beauty or to offer relaxation.

business or not, all estheticians need to promote themselves and market their services to clients.

Education and Training

Students who wish to follow this career path may take cosmetology courses in high school. A high school diploma (or equivalent) and a state-approved program are required in order to be an esthetician. Most esthetician courses are part of a larger cosmetology program that also includes classes on hair and nails. Programs are available at community colleges or cosmetology and beauty schools.

In addition to classes on skin care, hair removal, and makeup application, students also take courses in massage, customer service, safety and sanitation, and anatomy. Estheticians who plan to open their own business may also take salon management, sales, and marketing courses. Estheticians must continuously update their skills to keep up with the latest industry developments.

Programs, which can take anywhere from nine months to two years to complete, combine traditional classroom learning with hands-on practical skills. In almost all states, estheticians must have a license to practice. Depending on which state an esthetician wishes to practice in, licenses may be obtained by putting in a specified number of hours in school, through internships, or via apprenticeship programs—sometimes instead of completing a formal education program.

Licensing requires an exam, which can consist of both a written test and a demonstration of one's skills. For example, aspiring estheticians may need to demonstrate they know how to do a skin analysis or how to disinfect their tools properly. Some states require estheticians to renew their licenses, and some specializations—such as medical and oncology estheticians—may require advanced-level education and certifications. These professionals need to be familiar with medical conditions that affect the skin as well as know how to use specialized equipment such as lasers, which are used to treat certain skin conditions. Earning advanced certifications will provide more opportunities and increased pay. Some states, such as Washington and Utah, offer a master-level esthetician designation, which allows estheticians to perform higher-level services like microdermabrasion or chemical peels.

Because there are many career paths for an esthetician, it helps if students know in advance the setting in which they would like to work. "You could work on a cruise line and give facials there," suggests Rouleau. "You could work in a medical office, you could work in a skincare spa, you could work in a department store, you could be a sales rep for a skincare line." Above all, she advises students interested in this line of work to know where they might want to end up. "Before you go to school really have an understanding of where you would like to work," she says. "That way . . . you can always be making sure that you're learning the things that you'll need to work in that kind of environment."[7]

Skills and Personality

Estheticians have a unique skill set. Because they work directly with the public, they need to have excellent customer service skills. They need superior listening skills and must be able to communicate effectively. This is particularly important for attracting new clients and turning them into repeat clients.

Estheticians should also have strong critical-thinking skills. These are useful should an esthetician need to assess a client's skin type or the presence of any disorders or sensitivities—this helps determine the right care and products. Estheticians also need manual and finger dexterity to accurately and delicately apply skin care treatments and makeup. Physical stamina is important, too, since estheticians are on their feet most of the day.

Good organization and time-management skills are also crucial because estheticians juggle clients, appointments, and timed treatments. In addition, people working in this field need a working knowledge of sales and marketing, while self-employed estheticians need basic business skills.

Working Conditions

Most estheticians work full-time. Many, particularly those who work in salons or department stores, work both evenings and weekends—or whenever their clients are available to be seen. Self-employed estheticians have more flexibility in terms of being able to make their own schedules.

Because being an esthetician is physically demanding work, estheticians are at risk for potential health issues from standing or sitting for long periods or performing repetitive movements. They can also be exposed to harmful chemicals and acids (both topically and through inhalation) used in various skin care treatments and need to take safety precautions.

Employers and Pay

In 2018 the Bureau of Labor Statistics (BLS) reported that the number of skin care specialists, or estheticians, was close to seventy-two thousand. Almost 50 percent of this occupational group works in the personal care industry at salons, spas, hotels, and resorts. Close to 30 percent are self-employed. And a further 8 percent of estheticians work for dermatologists, surgeons, and oncologists. Some estheticians work as beauty school teachers, beauty magazine editors, or sales representatives for beauty product companies.

On average, estheticians make more than $31,000 per year, according to the BLS. And those who work in medical or surgical hospitals earn more than $46,000 on average. Estheticians who also have specialized certifications in techniques like laser hair removal, lash extensions, or microdermabrasion have more opportunities and higher pay. And many estheticians supplement their income by selling salon products.

What Is the Future Outlook for Estheticians?

According to the BLS, employment for estheticians is expected to grow by 11 percent through 2028. This is faster than the growth expected for all professions, and much of the increased demand will be due to the country's aging population—clients are looking for treatments to counteract the aging process. There is also an increased demand for treatments for people with medical conditions such as cancer. Plus, the number of salons is expected to increase due to a relatively new and growing market—men.

Find Out More

American Association of Cosmetology Schools (AACS)

website: http://beautyschools.org

The AACS is a national organization of privately owned cosmetology schools. Its website features a job bank as well as information on cosmetology schools, online training, grants, scholarships, and licensing and accreditation requirements by state.

Associated Skin Care Professionals (ASCP)

website: www.ascpskincare.com

The ASCP is a national organization for estheticians. Its website provides access to *Skin Deep* magazine. It also offers over one hundred on-demand industry webinars, liability insurance, and marketing resources, including a free website.

National Coalition of Estheticians, Manufacturers/Distributors & Associations (NCEA)

website: https://nceacertified.org/ncea-national-esthetician-association-associations

The NCEA provides information for estheticians on getting NCEA-certified in certain techniques and treatments. Certifications can help estheticians achieve standard industry practices, as well as obtain greater career opportunities.

Professional Beauty Association (PBA)

website: www.probeauty.org

The PBA is an association of salon professionals. Its website provides live educational events, resources, webinars, online on-demand training, and scholarship information for cosmetology students.

Nail Technician/Artist

What Does a Nail Technician Do?

A nail technician cleans, repairs, shapes, and stylizes a client's nails by applying polish, gel or acrylic nails, or extensions. Nail technicians who work exclusively on hands are also called manicurists, and those who work on feet are called pedicurists. Depending on the service, nail techs often massage a client's hands, arms, feet, and calves as well as remove any rough skin from a client's feet, if doing a pedicure. In addition, nail techs provide advice to clients on nail care and recommend products.

But that is only half the job. Nails have become a fashion accessory for some people—mini works of art. Nails are seen as an empty canvas, and the nail tech as the artist. And inspiration is everywhere. For example, after the 2019 Dolce & Gabbana runway show featured crocheted fashion, nail artists re-created the crocheted look on nails. Sarah Gibson Tuttle, the founder of Olive & June, a chain of luxury nail salons, tells *Glamour* magazine, "Having fun with your mani is back in, especially telling a story across a few nails."[8]

A Support Network

"Being a tech, you hear so many stories happy and sad. It's so much fun to be a part of a bride's special day, doing something special for a birthday, or helping someone relax after a loss/ stressful time. We aren't just techs we are friends, therapists, a support network."

—Hope Szymanski, nail technician

Hope Szymanski, "Eighteen Reasons Why Being a Nail Tech Is the Best Job Ever," *Nailpro*, November 13, 2014. www.nailpro.com.

And as technology develops, there are more and more interesting ways to tell those stories. Fingernails2Go is an example. This app allows people to choose designs from an extensive library or use their smartphone to design their own nail art from photos. The art is auto-sized to fit their nails, and then a specialized printer creates a set of artificial nails—in seconds. Bonnie Flanagan of Fingernails2Go says the app allows nail techs to provide a more personalized experience: "With technology advancements customers can experiment with designs to reflect their uniqueness and individuality."[9]

For nail techs who want to work in the entertainment field, a career as an editorial nail artist might be a good fit. These nail techs find work doing nails for models and actors for magazine spreads, fashion shows, red carpet premieres, TV or print ads, music videos, and even films. Naomi Yasuda, a celebrity manicurist whose clients include Lady Gaga and Madonna, says being an editorial nail artist offers variety, and unlike a salon, no two days are the same. Yasuda also finds the work creatively satisfying. "I love fashion and art, so it's incredibly rewarding to see my work on a billboard or in a magazine,"[10] she says.

Nail techs also employ creativity in how they attract customers. Some nail salons create unique experiences like providing clients drinks or headsets that play relaxing music. Bellacures, a franchise nail salon that is reportedly popular with actors such as

Reese Witherspoon and Jessica Alba, offers its clients a meditative and virtual reality experience while providing nail services. A client may be found relaxing with his or her feet in a foot bath while a headset transports them to a tropical beach in Hawaii. The meditative experience, complete with aromatherapy and relaxing music, engages the senses.

Owner Gerard Quiroga explains how Bellacures has transformed the salon experience. "Our clients come to Bellacures to unplug and escape. This service enhances that, as we are able to take them to beautiful, scenic locations and create a truly idyllic experience—almost like a mini vacation!"[11]

Other ways that some nail salons have transformed the industry include creating mobile salons, which allow the nail tech to travel to the client. Mobile services cater to bridal parties, bachelorette events, and birthday parties.

And, although men have been getting discreet manicures for years, they too are starting to see nails as an accessory. For example, rapper and style icon A$AP Rocky often shows off his nail art on Instagram. He shares with *Vogue* magazine, "I feel like men should be able to do nail art without feeling feminine."[12]

A Typical Workday for a Nail Technician

Nail techs spend most of their workday providing manicures and pedicures to clients. Cleaning and sanitizing their tools in between every client is a big part of their job. They may also schedule appointments and take payments for services. Some nail techs, particularly those who work for themselves, also need to order products and supplies as they use them up. If they also own their business and employ staff, they will need to hire, schedule, and supervise employees. Techs also may be required to do light bookkeeping as well as keep up with advertising and promote themselves, their services, and their work.

Education and Training

Nails are usually part of a cosmetology program, and students interested in this career field would do well to take cosmetology courses in high school, if they are offered. To be a nail tech, students need a high school diploma (or equivalent) and postsecondary education at a state-approved cosmetology school or nail tech program. Some states allow nail techs to learn their craft through apprenticeship programs.

Most programs take from nine to twelve months to complete. Programs include courses on the use of nail tools, nail health, and sterilization and hygienic techniques. Nail techs who plan to open their own salon may also take business, sales, and marketing courses. And techs who wish to specialize in the entertainment industry may need further training. Nail trends change constantly, so it is important that nail techs stay up-to-date on the latest styles and products. Doing this will provide more opportunities.

Following successful completion of a program or apprenticeship, nail techs are required to obtain a state license. Licensing varies from state to state, so it is important to know the requirements before choosing a school. Most states require nail techs to take a written and practical exam as part of the licensing process. Services such as mobile manicures and pedicures may require an additional license.

Few states offer licenses exclusively for nail techs. Most offer cosmetology licenses. Some states require nail techs to renew their license at set intervals. And some state boards will allow techs licensed in another state to get a license without retesting.

Those who want to work as editorial nail artists need a portfolio to show an art director or producer. Portfolios are generally online these days. Artists who are just starting out can offer their services for free to photographers in exchange for a photo shoot to obtain portfolio samples. Nail techs can also get agents to help them find editorial jobs. But regardless of career goals, it is important to show and promote their work on social media.

Julie Kandalec, celebrity manicurist to Emilia Clarke and Mariah Carey, explains, "Join Pinterest and create mood boards of images that inspire you—angles, lighting, nail shapes, models, unique art. Create a professional Instagram page and link it to a Facebook business page for the over-30 demographic."[13]

Skills and Personality

Because nail technicians work with the public, it helps if they enjoy talking to people, are good listeners, and are dedicated to providing excellent customer service. Those qualities, along with technical expertise, will help techs both build their reputation and establish repeat business.

Creativity is a must for nail techs. People in this industry need the ability to envision and create intricate designs. Nail techs also need manual and finger dexterity, since they work with small tools while giving manicures and pedicures. A steady hand with good eye-hand coordination and extreme attention to detail will help keep customers satisfied.

Finally, having business skills is always a plus for someone in this field. Performing administrative tasks like processing payments or doing paperwork can make a nail tech an invaluable part of a busy salon. Plus, after getting a few years' experience under their belts, many nail techs go on to open their own salons.

A nail technician cleans, repairs, shapes, and stylizes a client's nails. In addition, nail techs provide advice to clients on nail care and can recommend products.

Working Conditions

Nail techs may work part time or full time, and their hours may depend on their clients' schedule and availability. They often work evenings and weekends, since these are usually a salon's busiest times. Nail techs who work solely for celebrities must be available at any time for their clients.

Techs often sit all day. They also usually wear protective masks, gloves, and clothing to protect themselves from some of the harsh chemicals used in the course of their work.

Employers and Pay

According to the Bureau of Labor Statistics (BLS), nail techs held more than 156,000 jobs in 2018. Personal care services like salons or spas were the largest employers of nail techs, at 69 percent. Twenty-eight percent were self-employed.

The BLS states that the average wage for manicurists and pedicurists was $11.70 per hour in 2018. The lowest-paid 10 percent of nail techs earned less than $9.50, and the highest-paid 10 percent earned more than $16.00. This translates to about $20,000 to $34,000 per year.

Geographic location affects how much a nail tech can earn. Salons in large urban centers usually pay more. And editorial nail artists or those who work for celebrities can earn much more than the average. Nail techs can also earn tips plus commissions on the salon products they sell.

Expert Polish

"Artistic expertise has become an important part of creating nail art, but even if you can paint the *Mona Lisa*, no one will hire you if your polishing and cuticle work aren't impeccable."

—Elle, celebrity nail artist for Jennifer Lopez

Quoted in Francesca Moisin, "Behind the Bling," *Nailpro*, September 2019. www.nxtbook .com.

What Is the Future Outlook for Nail Technicians?

Job prospects for nail techs are increasing. The number of jobs in this field are expected to grow by 10 percent through 2028, according to the BLS. This is much faster growth than other industries and is expected to translate into another 15,700 jobs. Mobile nail services, as well as the increase in male clients, are helping drive employment in this sector.

Find Out More

American Association of Cosmetology Schools (AACS)
website: http://beautyschools.org

The AACS is a national organization of privately owned cosmetology schools. Its website features a job bank as well as information on cosmetology schools, online training, grants, scholarships, and licensing and accreditation requirements by state.

Associated Nail Professionals
website: www.nailprofessional.com

This site for professional nail techs has a student section that includes information on obtaining liability insurance and links to licensing information for nail techs by state. This membership-based organization also offers a free subscription to a nails magazine and a free and easy-to-use website builder so students can build and present their portfolio online while still in school.

Nailpro
www.nailpro.com

This magazine and blog features step-by-step tutorials, the latest nail trends, and business tips. The website also curates a user gallery, where nail artists can post their best looks and promote their Instagram accounts for a chance to appear in the magazine or blog.

Nails Magazine
www.nailsmag.com

This magazine's website offers information for nail techs such as industry news, trends, the latest nail techniques, best hygienic practices, and nail health. *Nails Magazine* also features competitions and has a section for students and nail professionals just starting out in the business.

Cosmetologist/ Spa Owner

What Does a Cosmetologist/ Spa Owner Do?

Most people think cosmetologists cut hair, paint nails, or perform facials. All of that is true—but many cosmetologists are also business owners. According to the Hair Professionals Career College website, "Many salon and spa owners are cosmetology school graduates. The people who own beauty schools are also cosmetology school grads more often than not."[14]

Owning a spa is lot of work and takes an entrepreneur's mind-set, but there are many rewards, including a possible six-figure income. Those interested in owning their own spas can buy a spa franchise (one of an already established chain) or open their own spa and either rent out space to hairstylists, estheticians, and nail technicians or have them work on a commission basis, whereby they earn a percentage of every sale made. Regardless of how one does it, a good way to become a spa owner is by becoming a cosmetologist first.

Spa owner Lori Crete got her start that way. She went to cosmetology school and specialized as an esthetician. She eventually opened her own spa, Spa 10, and almost two decades later she has several spas. In addition to being the owner and renting out spaces to others for a monthly fee, she still maintains her esthetician's license and offers services, including certified treatments for cancer patients.

Crete likes serving in both of these roles and finds them rewarding in different ways. She says:

> As an esthetician I love helping people achieve and maintain beautiful skin. I love making my clients look and feel beautiful. As a spa owner I love the fact that I provide others with a clean, friendly work environment where they can make money to provide for themselves and their family. I love the stability of knowing that I have a business of my own and really no one to answer to when decisions need to be made.[15]

Crete also earns money by selling a line of beauty products, speaking in public on topics such as leadership, and coaching other cosmetologists on how to create their own six-figure business.

Spas are as varied as the people who own them. Generally, spas offer their clients beauty treatments in a relaxing atmosphere, but there are many kinds of spas. For example, day spas are for daily appointments for clients who want to get a facial, a manicure, waxing services, airbrush spray tanning, or eyelash extensions. Vacation spas, on the other hand, are usually part of a hotel or resort. Clients who frequent these spas are usually guests of the venue and are looking to get pampered; that is, to rest and rejuvenate. These spas might also offer makeup application, nail services, hairstyling, and massage. Destination spas cater to people who travel specifically to experience the spa itself. These institutions might be focused on health, weight loss, fitness, or other curative wellness services like mineral springs. Finally, there are medical spas that are supervised by health care professionals and offer wellness services and therapies alongside medical treatments like cosmetic surgery.

They cater to people with specific medical issues, such as those who are burn victims or oncology patients.

A Typical Workday for a Cosmetologist/Spa Owner

A typical workday for cosmetologists and spa owners depends on whether they see their own clients or are responsible for running their spa. Those who are licensed as estheticians, nail technicians, or hairstylists will see clients for part of the day. Depending on their specialty, cosmetologists might do hair extensions or give a massage, facial, or manicure. In between clients, it is important that cosmetologists clean their work area and tools thoroughly. Rebecca Fletcher has been a cosmetologist for almost three decades and sees up to fifteen clients a day. "I'm mostly cutting hair and doing chemical processing, making people look beautiful," says Fletcher.

My appointments are often back-to-back, so my work tends to be fast-paced, and I'm on my feet all day. It takes an hour and a half to two hours for a chemical process [such as hair coloring] and half an hour for haircuts, so on a day when I'm just cutting hair, I see a lot of people![16]

The daily duties of spa owners, meanwhile, include tasks like dealing with maintenance or equipment repairs, ordering supplies or beauty products, and overseeing the staff or professionals who work at the spa. Spa owners typically collect payments or do some light bookkeeping like budgeting or sending out invoices and paying bills. They might have to hire, train, or fire individuals. Owners are also responsible for promoting their business, so they might spend time posting on social media or taking out ads.

Education and Training

Some high schools offer cosmetology courses, which would be a great start for anyone considering this as a career. Entrepreneur or business classes would also be an asset to those who would like to own a spa.

To be a cosmetologist, a high school diploma (or its equivalent) and a state-approved cosmetology program are required. Cosmetology programs cover three areas: skin care, makeup, and nails. Programs are available at community colleges, beauty schools, and cosmetology schools and combine traditional classroom learning with hands-on practice.

Students will take classes in hairstyling, nail health, skin care, color theory, customer service, nail and hair pathology, and sanitation and sterilization practices. Cosmetologists who plan to open their own spa may also take business, sales, and marketing courses.

Most certificate and diploma programs take up to a year to complete. The length of the program is determined by the number of hours required by the state licensing board. Almost all states require cosmetologists to be licensed and to take an exam. The exam includes both a written and a practical-skills test. Some states require cosmetologists to update courses and renew their license from time to time. Cosmetologists must keep up-to-date on the latest treatments, products, and trends in their business.

Skills and Personality

Cosmetologists need to be creative and have a great sense of style. They also need good communication skills—especially listening skills. Writer Trudy Brunot explains the importance of both listening and great customer service in building a salon's clientele on Chron, the online version of the *Houston Chronicle*.

> Hair salon, spa and nail salon customers often know what they want but cannot describe it well, putting a cosmetologist's listening skills to the test. Cosmetologists must be able to hear and interpret what clients tell them in order to meet their expectations.[17]

Physical skills are also required, including stamina, since cosmetologists are usually on their feet all day. Cosmetologists also need good time-management skills because they are often juggling clients, appointments, and timed treatments.

Working Conditions

Working in the cosmetology industry can be physically demanding. These professionals work both part time and full time, primarily on their feet. Their busiest times are evenings and weekends. Self-employed cosmetologists can set their own schedules but need to make themselves available when their clients are.

Cosmetologists can be exposed to toxic chemicals such as hair curling or hair straightener treatments. They sometimes wear protective gloves, clothing, or masks to protect themselves.

Employers and Pay

The Bureau of Labor Statistics (BLS) groups barbers, hairstylists, and cosmetologists into one occupational group. In 2018 this group held about 766,100 jobs. Forty-seven percent of cosmetologists and hairstylists work in the personal care industry at salons, spas, hotels, and resorts. Almost as many—44 percent—are self-employed.

A Growing Industry

"Get ready to work hard and reap many benefits! The beauty industry has hit the billion dollar mark and continues to grow. . . . If you devote time and energy you can build a wonderful place to work that can bring happiness, joy and lots of money into your life."

—Lori Crete, spa owner and esthetician

Quoted in JobShadow, "Interview with a Spa Owner/Esthetician," 2012. https://jobshadow .com.

The BLS states that the average wage for cosmetologists was approximately $25,000 in 2018. A cosmetologist's salary is dependent on location, industry, and experience. Larger cities usually mean larger salaries. The highest-paying industry was the personal care industry, whereas the lowest was retail. According to Hair Professionals Career College, many cosmetologists become instructors as they move up the ladder.

> Many [cosmetologists] choose to go back to school after gaining experience in the industry to become certified to teach others the tricks of the trade. It can be a fun and rewarding path for those who want to help others be successful in the beauty industry.[18]

Staying on top of the latest health and beauty trends increases opportunities for cosmetologists, as does having experience working across areas like skin, hair, and nails. People in this industry also make tips on top of their salaries as well as a commission on products sold, which can keep them motivated to improve their skills and earn more money. High-demand cosmetologists with a steady and loyal clientele often open their own businesses.

Spa owners can make over $100,000 per year and earn money several different ways. They may rent rooms to other beauty professionals. They can make a profit on the products they sell. And they can also usually see their own clients if they own their own spa. Says Crete, "Like any career I believe if it is your passion and you work hard at it—the sky is the limit!"[19]

What Is the Future Outlook for Cosmetologists/Spa Owners?

According to the BLS, there is expected to be an 8 percent increase in barbers, hairstylists, and cosmetologists through 2028. This will equal roughly sixty-four thousand new jobs in the United States.

Driving this growth (which is faster than the average for all occupations) are many factors, including the growing number of people seeking wellness and beauty treatments, particularly baby boomers. As members of this generation age, they are looking for services to counteract the aging process. There is also a need to replace cosmetologists who are retiring or leaving the industry.

These trends have been driving growth in the spa industry worldwide. According to the Global Wellness Institute (GWI), one of the leading sources for research in the area of wellness, this industry is expected to be worth $128 billion by 2022. In order to staff the increased number of spas, the GWI projects the industry will need an additional three hundred thousand spa workers and fifty-four thousand spa managers by 2022.

Find Out More

American Association of Cosmetology Schools (AACS)
website: http://beautyschools.org

The AACS is a national organization of privately owned cosmetology schools. Its website features a job bank as well as information on cosmetology schools, online training, grants, scholarships, and licensing and accreditation requirements by state.

Beauty Schools Directory

website: www.beautyschoolsdirectory.com

The Beauty Schools Directory, which lists over five hundred schools, can assist students interested in a cosmetology career in finding schools, state board requirements, scholarships, financial aid, accreditation, licensing information, and jobs.

Professional Beauty Association (PBA)

website: www.probeauty.org

The PBA is an association of salon professionals. Its website provides live educational events, resources, webinars, online on-demand training, and scholarship information for cosmetology students.

Spa Industry Association (SIA)

website: https://dayspaassociation.com

The SIA supports the Day Spa Association and the International Medical Spa Association and provides information and support for day spas, medical spas, resort spas, and spa professionals. Its website provides information on accreditation and certification, education, resources, industry news, spa job listings, and a blog.

Makeup Artist

What Does a Makeup Artist Do?

To be a makeup artist is to have a very creative career. Makeup artists paint and sculpt with color, and their clients' faces and bodies are their canvas. These artists get to experiment with different looks and sometimes create beauty trends.

Many makeup artists work in spas, salons, and retail settings, where they apply makeup, demonstrate application techniques, and recommend products to their clients. Some work in the hospitality business for hotels, resorts, and cruise ships, where they get to meet a lot of new people but encounter a different sort of clientele: "Don't get attached," warns Jackie Summers, a beauty writer for *Modern Salon* magazine. "You'll work on hotel guests or cruise ship passengers for the duration of their trip, then probably never see them again. The bonus for the cruise ship gig is traveling to amazing places—all for free!"[20]

Makeup artists can also be found working behind the scenes in the entertainment field. Some work on creative productions like plays, television

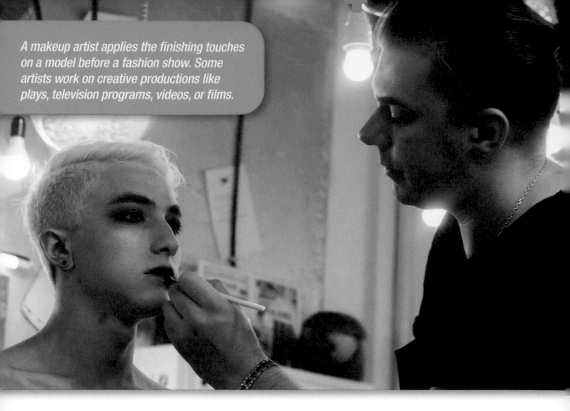

A makeup artist applies the finishing touches on a model before a fashion show. Some artists work on creative productions like plays, television programs, videos, or films.

programs, videos, or films, where they might apply wigs, prosthetic features, or makeup so actors can embody their character. Some work for magazines or photographers on fashion shoots, applying makeup to models. Some makeup artists become as famous as the celebrity clients they serve and are sought out to endorse products, write books about their experiences, or develop their own line of beauty products.

Carl Ray is one makeup artist who is known almost as well as his A-list clients, who include former First Lady Michelle Obama. Ray has been Obama's personal makeup artist for years, getting her ready for many magazine shoots, including ones for *Vogue* and *InStyle*. He also accompanied her on her tour for her 2018 book, *Becoming*. Ray likes to get to know his clients so he can use his brush to bring out both their beauty and their personality. Obama explains, "Carl genuinely wants to understand what makes a woman feel confident and radiant, and he builds on that."[21]

Some makeup artists work in various medical settings, performing services for cosmetic surgeons, dermatologists, and oncologists. In such environments, makeup artists work with people who have skin conditions, burn scars, or skin ravaged by the side effects of cancer treatments. Joy A. Johnson, owner of Nails & Faces of Joy, a mobile spa, is a makeup artist who works with this community. She created the Survive and Thrive program, which offers pampering and beauty treatments to cancer survivors. She got the idea after watching her mother, who was a fashion model, suffer from breast cancer. Johnson explains,

> I watched my mother's appearance deteriorate. If the pain of cancer treatment wasn't enough for one to go through, the physical changes and side effects that many patients experience—while battling the disease—heightens the trauma and struggle, especially for women who feel forced to abandon the joy of a beauty routine.[22]

A Typical Workday for a Makeup Artist

A typical day for makeup artists is in fact not typical at all and highly depends on where they work. Makeup artists who work in spas or salons usually work on an appointment system and see many clients a day. In between clients, it is important for artists to keep their work space and tools clean so they do not transmit bacteria or contagious skin conditions from client to client.

Self-employed or freelance makeup artists might need to perform light bookkeeping duties, such as booking appointments, invoicing clients, and tracking payments. They also need to maintain inventory and order products when they are running low. Regardless of whether they work for themselves or someone else, makeup artists need to spend time marketing and promoting themselves on social media to attract clients.

Celebrity makeup artist Katey Denno says if makeup artists want to be successful, it is crucial to have a web presence. "I didn't believe it until my then-agent gave me a stern talking to," Denno says. "Soon after, I launched my blog and landed a piece on *Vogue.com* about my favorite products. It was at that point

I realized how important it is to establish yourself as a brand in this industry, as well as establish a daily presence in the world of social media."[23]

Education and Training

Most makeup artist programs are part of a larger cosmetology program that also includes classes on skin care, hair, and nails. Most states require a makeup artist to have a high school diploma (or equivalent) and complete a state-approved postsecondary program to earn a cosmetology license. Some high schools offer cosmetology classes, which are a good introduction for students interested in working in this industry. Getting a job at a store's makeup counter provides great experience. John Stapleton, senior artist for M.A.C. Cosmetics, explains, "There you'll find a revolving door of personalities, skin types, ages, you name it. Customer service is a major aspect of makeup services, and the counter is the best place to get the most exposure and experience."[24]

Formal education is not always required for makeup artists who do not work in licensed establishments like spas or salons. Many artists learn through on-the-job training or by taking courses in various makeup application techniques. Licensing is also not necessarily required for makeup artists who work outside the spa or salon industry, such as those who work for retail, media, the military, theater, TV, film, photographers, doctors, or mortuary companies.

Cosmetology programs are available at community colleges and beauty schools, and most take nine to twelve months to complete. These programs combine traditional classroom lectures with practical hands-on work. In addition to classes on makeup application and color theory, cosmetology students will take classes in hairstyling, customer service, aesthetics, manicures, pedicures, massage, and sanitation and sterilization practices. Artists who plan to open their own business may also take business, sales, and marketing courses. Dedicated makeup artist schools may have specific career streams for those interested in beauty and fashion or TV, stage, and film.

In order to get work as a makeup artist, artists need to create a portfolio of their best work. A portfolio includes professional photos of people that the artist has worked on. Photos need to be professional looking, and it helps if the clients are professional models as well. Artists can display their portfolio on social media platforms such as Instagram to attract clients. Makeup artist Carolyn Berry explains, "It pays to invest in your portfolio. . . . Contact your local beauty photographers and pay them . . . to shoot your portfolio. Once you have amazing images, you will be able to attract more high-quality photographers to work with."[25]

Skills and Personality

The best makeup artists are creative. They also need to be friendly, since they work with the public. Good communication skills—especially listening skills—are important for successful client relationships. Finger and manual dexterity are also important—for example, when applying eyelash extensions. A makeup artist's clients probably have diverse skin tones, so artists need good organizational skills to keep track of multiple products in their makeup toolbox. These professionals also need a good knowledge of sales and marketing, especially those who are self-employed. Makeup artists need to advertise their artistry to attract clients.

Working Conditions

Makeup artists generally work both part time and full time and are always on their feet. Their busiest times are evenings and weekends. Self-employed artists can set their own schedules, but those who work in the entertainment industry should be prepared to work long hours and sacrifice their own personal time. Latonya Green, a personal makeup artist, has learned about this challenging side of the business firsthand. "You need to make yourself available 24 hrs a day," she says. "In order to keep regular clients, I have had to cancel on so many family functions, etc. If you don't make yourself available they will find another makeup artist who is. It's very hard to make plans for yourself."[26]

Employers and Pay

The Bureau of Labor Statistics (BLS) places makeup artists in the same category as cosmetologists, which are included with the same occupational group as hairstylists and barbers. In 2018 this group held more than 766,000 jobs.

Approximately 52 percent of this group works in the personal care industry, including salons, spas, hotels, and resorts. Many others—43 percent—are self-employed. Some work out of their homes, some rent space from salons, and some freelance. Freelancers work on location for bridal parties, photography and magazine shoots, the entertainment industry, or for private clients such as celebrities and models. Makeup artists could also find positions in related beauty industries. These include beauty school teaching jobs and sales representatives for beauty product companies.

Because their clientele and work environment can vary so much, makeup artists can earn anywhere from $22,000 to $130,000 per year (as reported by the BLS in 2018). The average annual wage for artists who work in the entertainment industry is $78,000. However, the majority of these jobs are based in California and New York, where the entertainment industry is focused.

What Is the Future Outlook for Makeup Artists?

Makeup artists are part of a growing industry. According to the BLS, there is expected to be an 8 percent increase in this occupational group (barbers, hairstylists, and cosmetologists) through 2028, which will result in about sixty-four thousand new jobs.

In addition to this growth, which is faster than the average, is the need to replace makeup artists who are retiring or leaving the industry. There is also a growing demand for artists who work in the entertainment business, particularly because of the increased demand for content on streaming platforms like Netflix and Amazon.

Find Out More

American Association of Cosmetology Schools (AACS)
website: http://beautyschools.org

The AACS, an organization of national, privately owned cosmetology schools, was founded in 1924. Its website features a career section, where students interested in a career as a makeup artist can find information on related schools, webinars, online training, licensing and accreditation requirements by state, grants, and scholarships.

Beauty Schools Directory
website: www.beautyschoolsdirectory.com

The Beauty Schools Directory, which lists over five hundred schools, can assist students in finding schools, state board requirements, scholarships, financial aid, accreditation, licensing information, and jobs.

Modern Salon

website: www.modernsalon.com

Modern Salon is a media group of beauty magazines that positions itself as a resource for beauty issues. Although its focus is primarily on the hair industry, it has a section for makeup artists, including a blog. The website also has links to licensing cosmetology boards for all US states.

Professional Beauty Association (PBA)

website: www.probeauty.org

The PBA is the largest association of salon professionals. Its website provides live educational events, resources, webinars, online on-demand training, and scholarship information for cosmetology students.

Massage Therapist

What Does a Massage Therapist Do?

Massage therapists use touch—primarily their hands—to manipulate the body's muscles and other soft tissues for therapeutic purposes, such as to relieve pain, release tension, and reduce stress. At one time massage therapy was considered an alternative treatment or was employed strictly for relaxation. However, more and more physicians are recommending massage to complement standard medical care. The Mayo Clinic, a nonprofit health care system, suggests that massage can help many ailments, including anxiety, insomnia, headaches, and muscle injuries. "Brush aside any thoughts that massage is only a feel-good way to indulge or pamper yourself," says the Mayo Clinic. "To the contrary, massage can be a powerful tool to help you take charge of your health and well-being, whether you have a specific health condition or are just looking for another stress reliever."[27]

Most massage therapists find their jobs rewarding, especially when working with clients with chronic or acute pain. Some therapists have found that massage can even help clients avoid turning to medications such as opioids, which are highly addictive. Some therapists use massage for clients who are nearing the end of their lives. Massage therapist Tracy Burkholder provides gentle massage for people in hospice, nursing homes, and assisted-living situations. Though she sometimes has to work around individuals' physical and cognitive challenges, Burkholder finds the work extremely gratifying. And her clients find that massage therapy can decrease depression and anxiety, as well as promote general well-being. "Massage can bring relief to the elderly suffering from isolation, anxiety and of course, the aches and pains of an experienced body."[28]

There are dozens of massage techniques. Some are designed to promote relaxation, such as those that feature hot rocks, aromatherapy, and candles. Others are intended to relieve pain, such as deep tissue massage or massage that takes place in a medical setting. Most massage therapists are skilled in several kinds of massage, and some are even trained to work with animals like dogs, cats, and horses. Equine massage therapists, for example, help horses with muscle tone, injuries, and especially relaxation, which can help improve a racehorse's performance.

Whether working with animals or humans, most massage therapists enjoy helping others. Monica Caulfield is often asked what drew her to a career as a licensed massage therapist. Her answer is always the same—compassion for others. "This quality seems to permeate the massage therapy business," she says. "For me, nothing is so powerful as understanding what is traumatizing a client and having the tools at my disposal to eliminate or significantly reduce their pain." Caulfield believes the best therapists truly care about helping their clients live better, pain-free lives.

A massage therapy career is not likely to bring you fame and fortune, [but] the joy and satisfaction that comes from helping people heal themselves has no boundaries. It is a thoroughly worthwhile endeavor for anyone with an abundance of compassion.[29]

A Typical Workday for a Massage Therapist

A typical day for massage therapists varies depending on their clientele. The bulk of their workday involves seeing clients, but how long each massage lasts can vary depending on the type of massage as well as the reason the client is getting a massage. For example, a relaxing spa-type massage typically lasts longer than an intensive massage for a sports injury. Massage therapists also spend time after each therapeutic appointment making notes about the client's condition and progress.

In between massages, therapists must thoroughly clean their work area and replace any towels or blankets used. Some therapists, especially those who are self-employed or have no staff, may spend a big part of their day doing laundry, since massage therapists go through a lot of linens. There are also some administrative tasks to attend to, such as returning calls, booking appointments, processing payments, and ordering supplies. In addition, these professionals need to allot time to market and promote themselves and their services, particularly on social media since massage is primarily a referral-based business.

Education and Training

Most states require massage therapists to have a high school diploma (or equivalent) plus complete a state-approved massage therapy program. Such programs are offered at certain types of colleges and dedicated massage schools. The length of a program depends on state requirements and includes both formal lectures and practical hands-on instruction. Courses may include anatomy, physiology, kinesiology, business skills, and ethics. Some of these subjects may be available at the high school level.

Most states require massage therapists to obtain a license or certification, which involves taking an exam—both a written one (in which they answer questions about the different kinds of massage, for example) and a practical one (in which they demonstrate their learned technique). Massage therapists may need to renew their license from time to time depending on which state they practice in. They may also be required to update their courses or certifications. Some states require that massage therapists be certified in cardiopulmonary resuscitation, and many states require that they undergo a background check by the police and retain liability insurance.

Skills and Personality

Massage therapists work with the public, so good interpersonal skills are a must. Compassion and patience are also needed, since therapists often work with people who are injured or in pain. Massage therapists need to be highly ethical as well, since they work in close contact with people. Respecting their client's privacy is also important, because sometimes therapists have access to private information and health records.

Physically, massage therapists need good manual and finger dexterity to massage clients. They need to be very strong, too, because giving massages is hard work. Says Lara Katsman, a massage therapist with more than twenty years' experience, "I . . . have superb physical stamina. I don't go to the gym, though. I work six days a week and I'm on my feet all day, I never sit and I'm always busy with my hands. My job is basically constant exercise."[30]

Working Conditions

Massage therapists work both part time and full time and often work more or less depending on their schedule and their personal lives. "Most of the time you can set your hours and have the flexibility to come and go as you please," says Caulfield.

This is the thing I love about being a massage therapist. . . . If I want to go on . . . vacation, I just mark off the time. If I want to work long hours before or after my vacation to catch up, I schedule this. If I want to see my child's play, I mark myself off for that time"[31]

Due to the physical nature of the profession, however, massage therapists are at risk of injuring themselves. For example, some get repetitive-motion injuries in their shoulders or wrists. And because they spend long hours on their feet, physical stamina is required for this physically demanding career.

Therefore, it is important that massage therapists take care of themselves as well as their clients. As Caulfield advanced in her career, she learned that she needed to take care of herself if she wanted to be her best self for her clients. She says, "To do excellent bodywork, the therapist has to be feeling 100% healthy in mind, body and spirit." Caulfield warns that this can sometimes be difficult to do.

Just try and do a full day of massage therapy with a runny nose, after an argument with your spouse or while you are worrying about paying your health insurance bill. To allow healing to take place for your client, it is imperative that the therapist is free of anxiety, stress, and worries and is feeling physically able to complete the treatment.[32]

Employers and Pay

According to the Bureau of Labor Statistics (BLS), there were approximately 160,000 massage therapist jobs in 2018. Thirty-three percent of massage therapists work in the personal care industry at places like spas, salons, cruise ships, resorts, wellness centers, and massage franchise companies. Twenty percent of massage therapists work in the health care industry for medical professionals such as doctors, physical therapists, or chiropractors, and 33 percent are self-employed. Some work out of their homes or a rented space, and some travel to their clients' homes or workplaces.

The average annual wage for massage therapists is $41,000. The lowest-paid 10 percent earn about $21,000, and the highest-paid 10 percent earn $78,000. Some can supplement their income with tips. Massage therapists who work in the personal care field generally earn less than those who work for chiropractors, for example; the latter average about $51,000 per year.

What Is the Future Outlook for Massage Therapists?

According to the BLS, employment for massage therapists is expected to grow by 22 percent through 2028, which is much faster than the average for all occupations. There are several reasons for this rapid growth. As massage becomes an increasingly popular way to treat various ailments, more physicians are referring patients to massage therapy. In turn, more health insurance companies are including massage as a covered service.

There has also been a growth in dedicated massage clinics, or franchises. In many spas and practices, massages are expensive, around ninety to one hundred dollars per hour. But franchised clinics generally offer massage services for about half that, which makes them much more affordable and thereby increases demand. And finally, the aging population has also resulted in a larger demand for massage therapy services.

Find Out More

American Massage Therapy Association (AMTA)
website: www.amtamassage.org

The AMTA is a national nonprofit organization for professional massage therapists. Its website features articles, online courses, resources, marketing tools, career guidance, and links to industry regulations by state.

Associated Bodyworks and Massage Professionals (ABMP)
website: www.abmp.com

The ABMP is a national association for bodywork and massage professionals. Its website offers career development information, videos of massage techniques and skills, a website builder, scholarship information, and a students' section with resources such as a test prep tool.

Commission on Massage Therapy Accreditation (COMTA)
website: www.comta.org

COMTA is an accrediting agency. It sets standards for educational institutions and programs for massage therapy and bodywork, as well as esthetics and skin care. Its website has a section for students featuring COMTA-endorsed schools, curriculum requirements, and scholarship information for students aspiring to have a career as a massage therapist.

MassageTherapyLicense.org
website: https://massagetherapylicense.org

This website provides information for students who may be considering a career as a massage therapist. It includes information on the licensing process, links to schools by state, and financial aid information.

Nutrition/Wellness Coach

A Few Facts

Pay
About $36,000 to
$96,000

**Educational
Requirements**
High school diploma
(or equivalent) plus
possible certifications or
associate's degree

**Personal
Qualities**
Good listening,
communication, and
motivational skills;
empathy

Work Settings
Gyms, fitness centers,
wellness centers, natural
food stores, resorts, and
spas

**Future Job
Outlook**
Growth of 11 percent
through 2028*

* Includes nutritionists and
dietitians

What Does a Nutrition/ Wellness Coach Do?

More and more people are concerned about what they eat and how it relates to their health and overall wellness. But with more food choices than ever and conflicting dietary advice, trying to determine what to eat and even when to eat it can be confusing. Neil Grimmer, founder of Habit, a personalized nutrition company, spoke about this dilemma at the 2018 Global Wellness Summit. "Since the dawn of time, we've been asking what foods are right for us," he said. "We've done high carb/low carb, high fat/low fat . . . one day eggs are good, the next they are bad. . . . The reality is that there's one prevailing question: 'what foods are right for me?'"[33]

This is where a nutrition coach comes in. A nutrition coach helps people find the foods and supplements that are right for them. They evaluate a client's lifestyle and eating behavior and help the client come up with a realistic, customized plan to follow. Then the nutrition coach motivates and supports the client in achieving his or her health goals. Because nutrition coaches have such a direct impact on their clients' health, it is a very rewarding career.

Lisa Bryan left the corporate world to become an online entrepreneur and nutrition coach. "The thing I love most about being a health coach is positively impacting clients and helping them reach their goals," she says. "It's almost a bonus that I get paid for doing so. We inspire, motivate and provide a level of accountability that is currently absent in the healthcare continuum. It's a 'missing link' that can provide enormous benefit."[34]

It is important to note that a nutrition coach is *not* a nutritionist or a dietitian. Those two occupational titles are career paths that require at least a bachelor's degree and sometimes advanced degrees. Nutrition coaches do not prescribe medications or order laboratory tests like blood work. They are not medically trained. In most states only nutritionists, dietitians, and physicians can recommend or prescribe nutritional advice to treat specific conditions like heart disease or diabetes. However, a nutrition coach can provide food or nutrition advice based on recognized resources from the government or the medical industry.

A Typical Workday for a Nutrition/Wellness Coach

A typical day for nutrition coaches varies. The majority of their time is spent consulting with clients. An initial consult with a new client in which the coach learns about the client's food history or health concerns could last from ninety minutes to two hours. Afterward, the coach designs a personalized, achievable eating plan for the client based on what the coach has learned.

At that point, the coach schedules a follow-up call with the client to go over the proposed nutrition plan. This session lasts approximately an hour. The coach might also schedule short check-in calls of fifteen to thirty minutes at regularly scheduled times to help support and motivate the client with his or her food goals.

Wellness coaches cover a broader health spectrum than nutrition coaches. A wellness coach might also consult on fitness as well as nutritional guidance. In addition, he or she may support clients with other healthy lifestyle changes like quitting smoking or reducing stress.

Nutrition coaches do not always work one-on-one. Some lead group coaching sessions for clients who are all focused on the same nutritional issue, such as living with diabetes or losing weight.

These specialized coaches need to spend time each day promoting themselves and their services on social media platforms because coaching is a referral business. Nutrition and fitness coach Mason Woodruff explains, "You should be posting about your personal journey and sharing information. People need to associate you with nutrition, food, fitness, and all things related to not being a couch potato."[35]

Education and Training

According to the Bureau of Labor Statistics (BLS), there are no recognized requirements for becoming a nutrition coach. However, having related training and certifications can give you an advantage over others in the field, increase your opportunities, and provide industry credibility. A high school diploma (or equivalent) may be needed to acquire certifications.

Students may take general life coaching courses through postsecondary institutions like community colleges and universities, as well as multiple online training and certification programs. Some programs may offer specific courses on nutrition coaching. However, the coaching field is unregulated in the United States. The BLS, which collects information on occupations, suggests that anyone who wants to follow a coaching career path do some research and connect with a credible coaching accreditation organization. According to the BLS, "Legitimate credentialing organizations, such as the International Coach Federation, evaluate programs based on specific standards of ethics and competency."[36] It is crucial that students interested in being a nutrition coach check their state's laws before enrolling in any program. Students can go to the Center for Nutrition Advocacy's website for more information.

Some states offer an associate of science degree in nutrition. Although this can provide a way into entry-level nutrition jobs like a nutritionist's assistant or a weight loss counselor, this career path is usually followed by those who want to eventually obtain a bachelor's or master's degree in nutrition, rather than to do coaching.

Prospective coaches should try to be mentored by a professional already working in the field. This can help aspiring coaches know what to expect of the job and gain confidence in their coaching techniques. "Getting the most out of your health coach certification program isn't just about completing your readings, watching your videos, and passing your tests," advises Bryan. "Perhaps the most important part? Practicing health coaching consultations with fellow students in your program—as many different people as possible."[37]

Skills and Personality

A nutrition coach's job is to help clients obtain their health goals. To that end, coaches need excellent listening, communicating, and motivating skills. They need to have a desire to help others.

Also, coaches work very closely with their clients and so must be empathetic; the more open-minded and nonjudgmental a coach is, the more he or she will be able to build rapport and connect deeply with clients.

Good nutrition coaches also need to be able to ask their clients very specific, detailed questions about their preferences, habits, lifestyles, and environments. This helps the coaches learn what might be preventing clients from meeting their food and health goals. The International Sports Sciences Association asserts that knowing the right questions to ask is a crucial quality for an effective nutrition coach. "Before developing a nutrition plan, start asking questions and go beyond the basics," the organization writes on its website.

> A good coach gets down to the 'why.' Why is losing weight important to you, or why are you ready to start eating healthier? The better your questions, the more information you'll uncover, and the better you'll be able to get people to their goals and see the weight loss results they're looking for.[38]

Working Conditions

Nutrition coaches can work either part time or full time. Being a coach is a very flexible job, particularly for the self-employed, who make their own schedules. Coaching can also be done in person or online. Many self-employed coaches consult with their clients online using face-to-face conferencing software like Skype, Zoom, or FaceTime.

Many coaches risk stress or burnout because they often give too much of their time and energy to their clients, who are sometimes very needy. Clients are often vulnerable when they share the personal details and struggles in their lives, and coaches need to be wary of not taking on a client's problems. Coaches need to set clear boundaries as to what is acceptable in the coach-client relationship and what is not. Coaches also need to practice self-care because of the giving nature of their job.

A Revolution in Health Care

"The health coach fills this new role that makes up for the doctor who just gives you Valium without having a conversation with you, the nutritionist who calorie counts, and the therapist who wants to dig into childhood and never talk about next steps. That stuff is so antiquated. We're moving into a place where we're taking responsibility for our health and happiness."

—Jennifer Kass, health coach

Quoted in Lisa Elaine Held, "The Coming of the Health Coach Revolution," Well and Good, November 15, 2012. www.wellandgood.com.

Employers and Pay

Most nutrition coaches are self-employed. Some work out of a rented office, while others have a dedicated office space in their home. Still other coaches may work for a corporation that offers a wellness program as part of its employee health benefits, while others work for gyms, fitness centers, wellness centers, natural food stores, resorts, and spas.

Coaches' salaries vary. Salary.com, which gathers data from human resource departments and employee compensation surveys, reported in September 2019 that nutrition coaches make $36,000 to $47,000 per year. The specific salary depends on a coach's certifications, education, and experience in the industry, and a good coach can charge as much as $100 per hour. Nutrition coaches who have an associate's degree earn approximately $89,000 to $96,000.

There are also numerous opportunities for nutrition coaches to supplement their income by writing books, speaking professionally on their topic, holding webinars, teaching at nutrition schools, creating a product line, or even opening their own restaurant. Nutrition coach Lisa Bryan built Downshiftology, a six-figure health and nutrition coaching business, through speaking, blogging, and writing books. "It took heaps of tenacity, long-hours and hard work, pursuing something I was unwaveringly passionate about.

But . . . nothing I've done in the last three years required any special connections, advanced degrees or extraordinary monetary investments. There was no secret sauce or private member club. Nope. None. In other words—it's all replicable."[39]

What Is the Future Outlook for Nutrition/Wellness Coaches?

The BLS projects much faster growth for dietitians and nutritionists than the average for all professions—11 percent through 2028. It follows that there would be similar growth for nutrition coaches. The coaching profession in general is growing and achieving more credibility. In addition, more businesses are offering workplace wellness programs to help their employees prevent disease. Some companies even subsidize (pay for a portion of or offer as part of a job's benefits) health coaching for their employees.

This lines up with findings from the BLS, which reports an increased trend toward preventive health care, particularly in regard to food and nutrition. New clients for nutrition coaches will also be found in the aging baby boomer population, since that generation will increasingly demand nutritional advice as a way to stay healthier longer.

Find Out More

Athletics and Fitness Association of America (AFAA)

website: www.afaa.com

The AFAA offers certifications and recertifications for nutrition coaches. The AFAA website features a blog, professional resources, workshops, continuing education courses, exam information, and a job board.

Center for Nutrition Advocacy

website: www.nutritionadvocacy.org

This organization seeks to transform the health of Americans by creating a system that is inclusive of all nutrition professionals regardless of their level of education. Its website offers up-to-date regulatory information for nutrition practitioners by state.

Institute for Integrative Nutrition (IIN)
website: www.integrativenutrition.com

The IIN is an online learning platform. According to its website, the IIN is the largest nutrition school in the world. The IIN offers programs in nutrition and health coaching. The website contains webinars and a blog featuring recipes and articles about health trends.

International Coach Federation (ICF)
website: https://coachfederation.org

The ICF is a global organization dedicated to advancing the coaching profession by setting and providing accredited core competency coaching standards worldwide. Nutrition coaches can get professional and advanced certifications in coaching skills such as listening, communication and ethics. The ICF website also offers tools and resources to help professional coaches succeed, including a research information portal.

Fitness Instructor

What Does a Fitness Instructor Do?

Fitness is a booming industry. According to a 2019 report, the global health and fitness club market was valued at more than $94 billion in 2018 and is expected to surpass $147 billion by 2024. This translates into an increased demand for fitness instructors.

Fitness instructors lead groups of people in exercise activities. They instruct participants on how to do a particular routine and motivate them to keep going during class. Routines can include cardiovascular workouts such as water aerobics, Zumba, or spin classes (which involve exercising on a stationary bicycle); strength-training sessions such as kettlebell, kickboxing, or Pilates; and stretching exercises such as yoga, barre, or aerial fitness.

Fitness instructors work with all kinds of people regardless of their age or level of fitness and adapt exercises as required for their clientele. They may choose to work with specific groups like teens, seniors, or those with medical or mobility challenges such as cancer or arthritis.

It is key that fitness instructors plan exercise routines that fit the goals of the class. This involves choreographing an appropriate routine and creating a playlist of music that is well timed with the movements. Group fitness instructor Mallory Creveling considers leading a class to be one part public speaker, one part teacher, one part motivator, and one part DJ. She says:

> Like the exercises I plan for a class, some days I know exactly what I want to include on a soundtrack; other days, it takes me an hour to find that one song I'm looking for. Some days the playlist works out perfectly; other times, the music slows down when I actually needed it to speed up. At the end of the day, it's a lot of trial and error—both the music and the overall experience—and every time, I start to get the hang of it a little more.[40]

Fitness classes need to evolve to keep the participants' interest and reflect new trends, which are always emerging. Some of popular classes in the past couple of years include circus-inspired aerial classes that combine yoga moves with being suspended from hoops and ropes; unstructured African-inspired Bokwa classes, in which participants draw numbers and letters with their feet in between fun dance moves; and Latin dance–inspired Zumba or Bollywood-inspired BollyX classes that provide lively, fast-paced workouts to specific styles of music.

Even traditional forms of exercise are getting makeovers from fitness instructors. Yoga, for example, can be done in numerous ways. There is hot yoga (done in a room warmed to 100°F, or 38°C), Yogilates (yoga combined with Pilates,) or chair yoga (yoga for people with mobility challenges). Still other classes like Date-ercise, a cross between speed dating and a circuit-type fitness class, are intended to make exercising more social. "Date-ercise is just like any other fitness class, with the twist that everyone is single and wanting to meet somebody,"[41] says Keith Mcniven, the creator of this trend.

A career as a fitness instructor can be very rewarding, as instructor Jessica Matthews explains:

> As a group fitness instructor for the past 18 years, I've had the pleasure of witnessing firsthand just what a unique opportunity group fitness classes provide for people to come together and experience movement in positive, memorable and purposeful ways. Group-based classes can be truly transformative when designed and led with the right intentions, helping to inspire meaningful change in individuals not just physically, but also mentally, emotionally and spiritually.[42]

A Typical Workday for a Fitness Instructor

The bulk of a fitness instructor's day is spent leading classes. In between classes, instructors need to set up their room or studio with the appropriate equipment. Fitness instructors then must come up with a routine of exercises that will challenge their clients and provide them with the desired physical results. This means that instructors need to have a clear plan for which moves they will present and the specific sequencing of the moves. Fitness instructor Beverly Hosford recognized this too late. "I didn't rehearse timing for the first class I ever taught back in 2005 and finished the 30-minute workout in 10 minutes!" she remembers. "However, this taught me to be adaptable and ready for anything—a skill that's essential for any teacher of groups."[43]

Finally, fitness instructors perform light administrative work such as making class schedules and writing course descriptions. They are also responsible for marketing their classes online via various social media channels. And if a fitness instructor also owns a studio or business, then he or she must take care of basic business tasks such as invoicing clients, processing payments, and doing other bookkeeping.

A Sense of Community

"When I first starting teaching group exercise, I thought participants wanted instructors who could cue perfectly and stay on the musical beat and phrase. As I matured as an instructor, I realized that those skills are only tangentially important to the group exercise experience. Participants join fitness classes for many reasons, but I have found that what keeps them coming back is a feeling of belonging, regardless of their skill level or fitness abilities. One of the most important things an instructor can do is to help every person feel that he or she belongs in the class."

—Amanda Vogel, group fitness instructor

Quoted in American Council on Exercise, "What I've Learned as a Group Fitness Instructor," January 23, 2018. www.acefitness.org.

Education and Training

A high school diploma (or equivalent) is usually the minimum educational requirement for most fitness instructors to work. Some employers require instructors to have specific certifications or an associate's degree in exercise science, physical education, or kinesiology. Some gyms look for fitness instructors with more advanced degrees. Students working on an associate's degree should expect to take classes in biology, anatomy, exercise techniques, and nutrition. Most formal educational programs take up to two years to complete.

There are different educational and certification requirements depending on what a fitness instructor plans to specialize in. Most employers prefer to hire instructors with both experience and certifications in the type of class they will teach, such as yoga. Some employers do not require program certifications.

However, fitness instructors are required to have certifications in cardiopulmonary resuscitation and automated external defibrillators. All certification programs require testing of the subject matter. The exam generally has a written portion and a practical-

The Best Instructors Are Also Students

"Exercise science is a constantly evolving field. In order to ensure that your students receive the safest and most effective class experiences, you must understand that not only will you be teaching classes, you'll also be taking classes (workshops, conference sessions, online courses, webinars, etc.) to be the best instructor you can be."

—Jessica Matthews, group fitness instructor

Quoted in Jessica Smith, "6 Things to Consider Before Becoming a Fitness Pro," *Shape*, 2019. www.shape.com.

skills test to demonstrate that the instructor knows the exercise techniques and their effect on the human body.

Skills and Personality

Fitness instructors need a special skill set. They need to have great motivational and communication skills to inspire and motivate their clients, especially when a client might want to give up mid-class. Jessica Smith of *Shape* magazine says fitness professionals have to be master motivators. She explains:

> Getting your client to finish those last few reps of a tough exercise, or simply motivating your students just to come back to the gym is no easy feat. Not everyone responds well to a drill sergeant training style, while others hate to be coddled, so finding a balance of motivational skills that are unique to you, your message, and your clients is going to be vital to your success in this field.[44]

Fitness instructors also need good time-management skills. They need to gauge the length of their classes and routines. They also need to be physically fit themselves, since it can be challenging to give instructions to a class and demonstrate movements at the same time. Stamina is also important, since instructors must lead several classes throughout a day, sometimes back-to-back.

Although many people think fitness instructors are fortunate to get to work out for free, Caroline Dawson, the managing director of Instructor Toolbox, a New York company that trains fitness instructors, disagrees. "At the end of the day, after working in a gym, the last thing you'll want to do is stay for a personal workout. Motivating yourself can be challenging when you're teaching (or training) often,"[45] she says.

Working Conditions

Fitness instructors may work part time or full time and may lead classes very early in the mornings, late in the evenings, and/or on weekends—whenever their clients are available to work out. If they teach for a gym or wellness center, they may work whenever they can pick up classes. However, those who are self-employed or have their own studios have more flexibility, but they should still expect to put in long hours. Dawson explains,

> It's easy to forget that being a group fitness instructor (or a personal trainer) is a job. That often means arriving early for class (and staying late to help students or clean up studios), and hours of preparation to research music, choreography, the science of what you're teaching, etc.[46]

Self-care is important for fitness instructors. It is a physically demanding job and takes a toll on the body, especially a person's joints. There is also a potential for physical injuries, including repetitive motion injuries, so instructors must take care to perform exercises correctly.

Employers and Pay

Fitness instructors find employment at fitness and wellness centers, recreation centers, pools, gyms, private studios, resorts, retreats, continuing education institutions, and even cruise ships. There were 357,000 jobs in 2018, according to the Bureau of Labor Statistics (BLS), and these include fitness or personal trainers. Fifty-eight percent of these workers worked for fitness or recreational centers, while only 11 percent reported being self-employed.

The BLS reports that this occupational group earns anywhere from $20,000 to $76,000, with a median annual salary of approximately $40,000. Fitness instructors who work for gyms or recreational centers generally earn more than the average.

What Is the Future Outlook for Fitness Instructors?

The BLS projects that there will be a 13 percent growth through 2028 for fitness instructors. That translates into about forty-six thousand more jobs. Some of these job opportunities will replace workers retiring or leaving the industry, but also fueling this growth is the fact that more and more businesses and even the government are recognizing that fitness can prevent and lessen the effects of illness and disease. As a result, more workplaces and insurance companies are providing incentives to join gyms or covering the cost of a fitness plan as part of an employee's health benefits. Some companies are even opening employee wellness studios on their premises. The fitness industry has seen steady growth in the past few years, particularly in regard to the aging baby boom generation. This group knows the benefit of being fit as a way to stay healthy in later years.

Find Out More
American College of Sports Medicine (ACSM)
website: www.acsm.org

The ACSM is an association for professionals in sports medicine, exercise science, and health and fitness. Its website provides certification (and recertification) information, a job bank, a resource library, and continuing education courses for health and fitness professionals.

American Council on Exercise (ACE)
website: www.acefitness.org

ACE, the only organization that offers a Health Coach Certification program accredited by the National Commission for Certifying Agencies, offers certification for fitness professionals.

Athletics and Fitness Association of America (AFAA)
website: www.afaa.com

The AFAA offers certifications and recertifications for group fitness instructors. The AFAA website features a blog, professional resources, workshops, continuing education courses, exam information, and a job board.

National Exercise Trainers Association (NETA)
website: www.netafit.org

NETA is a professional association for exercise trainers in the United States. NETA's website includes information for certifications and recertifications for fitness instructors, as well as specialty training in specific fitness classes. The site also offers continuing education courses, a blog, resources for instructors, and employment opportunities.

Personal Trainer

A Few Facts

Number of Jobs
About 357,000 in 2018*

Pay
About $20,000 to $76,000

Educational Requirements
High school diploma (or equivalent) and certification; some employers require associate's degree (or higher)

Personal Qualities
Motivational, interpersonal and customer service skills, physically fit

Work Settings
Fitness centers, private studios, gyms, recreation centers, clients' homes

Future Job Outlook
Growth of 13 percent through 2028*

* Includes fitness instructors

What Does a Personal Trainer Do?

Personal trainers work with clients, either one-on-one or in small groups, to help them meet their fitness goals. Through a health assessment and consultation, trainers assess their client's current fitness level and goals, then determine how to help them get there. Then they create personalized fitness and nutrition plans based on their clients' health objectives and skills. Trainers typically work with clients of all ages, skill levels, and abilities, and some work with specific groups like athletes, new mothers, senior citizens, or bodybuilders.

Each day, personal trainers demonstrate exercises and routines to their clients. They inspire and motivate clients to push past any resistance and achieve their goals. Exercises could be aerobic in nature, intended to exercise the heart and lungs; be strength-based, to build muscle and weight; or simply consist of gentle stretches, for better flexibility and balance.

Trainers help clients perform their routines correctly and safely to minimize their potential for getting hurt.

Each client's progress is monitored and sometimes adapted depending on the results. Seeing clients' results and improving their overall outlook is typically the most rewarding part of being a personal trainer; this is what trainer Jessie Newell loves best about the job. "I learned that you have the power to make someone's day!" she says. "Whether it's providing genuine, heartfelt feedback about their progress, complimenting their hard work, or simply offering a smile and a pat on the back, you can really boost someone's day."[47]

A Typical Workday for a Personal Trainer

Personal trainers spend most of their time working with clients either one-on-one or in small groups. This might include demonstrating a routine, showing how to perform an exercise or use a machine safely, monitoring clients' performance, or offering guidance. At other times a trainer and client may discuss training goals, which might include losing 20 pounds (9kg) or being able to lift a certain amount of weight.

When not working directly with clients, trainers are usually busy preparing to work with them, which involves setting up equipment for a session or reviewing a client consultation to create a personalized fitness or nutrition plan.

Personal trainers are part-time salespeople who sell training sessions. As such, trainers spend time networking and promoting their services (along with the gym with which they are affiliated), particularly on social media platforms. Trainers who own their own gym or studio may spend time doing light paperwork like billing clients and processing payments. Some trainers also answer phones, return calls, make appointments, and order supplies as part of their daily routine.

Education and Training

It is possible to become a personal trainer with only a high school diploma (or equivalent). But most employers require certifications as well as postsecondary education. Some personal trainers have a bachelor's or master's degree in physical education, health science, or kinesiology, but some only have an associate's degree. Students working toward an associate's degree (which generally takes two years to complete) might take classes in biology, anatomy, exercise techniques, and nutrition.

Some employers will hire personal trainers who do not have a postsecondary education but possess a combination of certifications and experience. Students going this route need to make sure their certification programs are accredited by the National Commission for Certifying Agencies (NCCA), since most employers prefer NCCA-accredited trainers.

Personal trainers are required at a minimum to have certifications in cardiopulmonary resuscitation and automated external defibrillators. An exam is administered for each certification to demonstrate mastery of the subject. This usually includes a written test and a practical skills test. Certification programs can take days or months.

It should be noted that most employers will also require trainers to have liability insurance in the event a client is injured as a result of training. Most insurance companies require trainers to have certifications to demonstrate they have the correct level of knowledge.

Personal trainers are their own brand, so it is important that they continue to educate themselves on the latest fitness and nutrition trends. Christopher Huffman, a personal trainer and gym owner, explains,

> Regardless of whether or not a trainer owns their own studio or gym, they still are the main representative of their own 'brand.' This requires experience and excellence in customer service, sales, and marketing if you are to expect continued success. You are your own billboard, brand ambassador, and business staff rolled into one.[48]

Skills and Personality

Personal trainers need specific skills to be effective at their job. Most importantly, these professionals need to be able to motivate and inspire their clients to meet their fitness goals. Trainers need to listen to their clients as well as communicate clearly so they can

A personal trainer instructs a client on the proper way to use weights. Through a health assessment and consultation, trainers assess a client's current fitness level and goals, then determine how to help them get there.

instruct them properly. They need to find a balance between being friendly and being firm to get the results their clients demand. And because personal trainers work with the public (and depend on them for their jobs), they need to have great customer service skills. They also need to manage their time well, since they must juggle multiple clients and appointments throughout the day.

Personal trainers also need to be in good physical shape, but not just because they put in long workdays. Trainers are a walking advertisement for their business. According to the National Federation of Professional Trainers, a trainer's appearance is important. "You don't have to be a supermodel or 'huge' or even 'buff' to be a personal trainer, despite what your inner ego tells you. But you DO have to 'walk the talk.' Being put together and looking like you care about yourself is something that people notice."[49]

Finally, good personal trainers need to be very patient, since their job can be quite frustrating at times. Their clients may not follow their training plan or may cancel appointments at the last minute.

Working Conditions

A personal trainer's schedule is tied to his or her clients. Trainers work both part time and full time, and they tend to be busiest in the evenings and on weekends, when clients who work more traditional schedules have time to work out. They also work long, strenuous days. "The hours can be absolutely grueling, namely due to the most demanded time slots in a typical workday schedule (early AM before work, late PM after work)," says Huffman. "Client cancellations and reschedules typically make for completely upended schedules week to week, making it difficult to have a normal schedule and social life."[50]

It can also be difficult to take time off when clients have scheduled appointments or are counting on their trainer to see them through a specific goal they have set. Add to this that a personal trainer must constantly work to attract a rotation of clients, marketing and promoting themselves, as well as keep up with new fitness trends.

The pressure and hard work connected with being a trainer can take a toll on a trainer's own health, so they must guard against burnout. Jeff Bell, a personal trainer and owner of a fitness company in New York City, says actually becoming a personal trainer is the easy part. "The hard part is creating a sustainable business that doesn't absorb all of your physical and emotional energy trying to get clients."[51]

Employers and Pay

The Bureau of Labor Statistics (BLS) reports that there were 357,000 jobs for personal trainers and fitness instructors (the same occupational group) in 2018. Almost 60 percent of these professionals worked for fitness or recreation centers, with 11 percent identifying as self-employed. Others travel to their clients' homes.

According to the BLS, fitness trainers and instructors make from $20,000 to $76,000, with a median annual salary of $40,000. Personal trainers generally earn some of the higher incomes—particularly those who work for gyms or recreation centers. Self-employed personal trainers can set their own rates. Income in this business is directly related to being able to attract and retain clients.

Huffman shares the following advice for those looking to succeed in the personal training industry: "Success [in] this career is based on overall reputation for providing results, having a compatible personality with a given client-base, and providing a level of service above and beyond others in the field. This allows a trainer to charge 'what they are worth' while clients recognize the value they are getting behind that premium."[52]

What Is the Future Outlook for Personal Trainers?

According to IBISWorld, a global market research company, the US personal training market was worth more than $9 billion in 2019 and is projected to grow. This is great news for current personal trainers and those who want to get into this field. And the BLS expects this industry to grow by 13 percent through 2028, which will result in approximately forty-six thousand more jobs.

As always, some of these new jobs are due to attrition of workers who are retiring or leaving the personal trainer industry. But this field is also growing due to the recognition of fitness as a way to prevent disease and illness. Some employers are including gym memberships as part of their employee benefits package. Likewise, insurance companies are offering their clients similar incentives. And as the US population ages, many people are seeking personal trainers as a way to stay fit, healthy, and prepared for their senior years.

Find Out More

American College of Sports Medicine (ACSM)

website: www.acsm.org

The ACSM is an association for professionals in sports medicine, exercise science, and health and fitness. The ACSM's website provides certification (and recertification) information, a job bank, a resource library, and continuing education courses for health and fitness professionals.

International Coach Federation (ICF)
website: https://coachfederation.org

The ICF is a global organization dedicated to advancing the coaching profession by setting and providing accredited coaching standards worldwide. The ICF website offers tools and resources to help professional coaches succeed, including a research information portal.

National Academy of Sports Medicine (NASM)
website: www.nasm.org

The NASM offers a certified personal trainer program as well as various related specializations. Its website features information on certifications, continuing education, recertifications, career guidance, and material on how to become a personal trainer.

National Exercise Trainers Association (NETA)
website: www.netafit.org

NETA is a professional association for exercise trainers in the United States. NETA's website includes information for certifications and recertifications for personal trainers as well as specialty training in various fitness styles. The site also offers continuing education courses, a blog, resources for trainers, and employment opportunities.

Source Notes

A Growing Industry

1. Quoted in Brand Minds, "The Health & Wellness Industry Is Now Worth $4.2 Trillion," Medium, April 26, 2019. https://medium.com.
2. Quoted in Selena Fragassi, "Tips for Waxing Newbies from Chicago's First Male Esthetician," Beautylish, January 6, 2014. www.beautylish.com.
3. Quoted in VoyageChicago, "Meet Julio Mendez of Wax Man Spa in Ravenswood," May 8, 2017. http://voyagechicago.com.
4. Quoted in VoyageChicago, "Meet Julio Mendez of Wax Man Spa in Ravenswood."

Esthetician

5. Quoted in Mary Nielsen, "Interview with Becky Kuehn, Oncology Spa Solutions," Milady Pro, March 21, 2017. www.miladypro.com.
6. Quoted in Renée Rouleau Skincare, "An Interview with Celebrity Esthetician, Renée Rouleau," YouTube, November 29, 2010. www.youtube.com/watch?v=OSoUPflGGQE.
7. Quoted in Renée Rouleau Skincare, "An Interview with Celebrity Esthetician, Renée Rouleau."

Nail Technician/Artist

8. Quoted in Bella Cacciatore, "Every L.A. Girl Is Obsessed with Star Nails This Summer," *Glamour*, July 16, 2019. www.glamour.com.
9. Quoted in *Nails Magazine*, "New Printer Uses HP Technology to Apply Nail Art," September 9, 2019. www.nailsmag.com.
10. Quoted in Francesca Moisin, "How to Make Your Mark as an Editorial Nail Tech," *Nailpro*, September 11, 2019. www.nailpro.com.

11. Quoted in Angelina Lewis, "Bellacures Introduces a Virtual Reality Salon Experience," *Nailpro*, August 13, 2019. www.nailpro.com.
12. Quoted in Luke Leitch, "Babushka Boi: A$AP Rocky on His New Store, Creativity, and the Real Reason He Started Wearing a Headscarf (Before Everyone Else Did)," *Vogue*, October 2, 2019. www.vogue.com.
13. Quoted in Francesca Moisin, "Behind the Bling," *Nailpro*, September 2019. www.nailpro.com.

Cosmetologist/Spa Owner

14. Hair Professionals Career College, "What Does a Cosmetologist Do?," July 21, 2017. https://hairpros.edu.
15. Quoted in JobShadow, "Interview with a Spa Owner/Esthetician," 2012. https://jobshadow.com.
16. Quoted in CareerColleges.com, "Interview with Cosmetologist, Rebecca Fletcher." www.careercolleges.com.
17. Trudy Brunot, "List of Cosmetology Quality & Character Traits," Chron, 2019. https://work.chron.com.
18. Hair Professionals Career College, "What Does a Cosmetologist Do?"
19. Quoted in JobShadow, "Interview with a Spa Owner/Esthetician."

Makeup Artist

20. Jackie Summers, "Beauty Industry Career Options," Beauty Changes Lives. https://beautychangeslives.org.
21. Quoted in *InStyle*, "6 Products Michelle Obama's Makeup Artist Swears By," December 10, 2018. www.instyle.com.
22. Quoted in Anne Moratto, "Cancer Patients Finding Pampering and Healing Go Together," *Modern Salon*, September 3, 2019. www.modernsalon.com.
23. Quoted in Valerie Tejeda, "How to Become a Makeup Artist: Advice from Top Professionals," *Teen Vogue*, December 20, 2017. www.teenvogue.com.
24. Quoted in Tejeda, "How to Become a Makeup Artist."

25. Quoted in "From the Mind of a Makeup Artist: What I Wish I Had Known Before Starting Out," makeupartistbeauty.com.
26. Quoted in "From the Mind of a Makeup Artist."

Massage Therapist

27. Mayo Clinic, "Massage: Get in Touch with Its Many Benefits," October 6, 2018. www.mayoclinic.org.
28. Quoted in MassageTherapyLicense.org, "Tracy Burkholder, LMT: Providing Massage to People at Different Stages of Life." https://massagetherapylicense.org.
29. Monica Caulfield, "Succeeding as a Professional Massage Therapist: What I Wish I Had Known and Some Tips," MassageTherapyLicense.org. https://massagetherapylicense.org.
30. Quoted in Harling Ross, "What Your Massage Therapist Is Actually Thinking," Man Repeller, December 8, 2017. www.manrepeller.com.
31. Caulfield, "Succeeding as a Professional Massage Therapist."
32. Caulfield, "Succeeding as a Professional Massage Therapist."

Nutrition/Wellness Coach

33. Quoted in Cassandra Cavanah and Beth McGroarty, "Nutrition Gets Very Personalized," Global Wellness Summit, 2019. www.globalwellnesssummit.com.
34. Lisa Bryan, "Should You Become a Health Coach? 4 Things to Consider," Downshiftology, November 11, 2017. https://downshiftology.com.
35. Mason Woodruff, "How to Become a Nutrition Coach," *Kinda Healthy Recipes* (blog), July 27, 2018. https://masonfit.com.
36. Quoted in Kathleen Green, "You're a What? Life Coach," Bureau of Labor Statistics, January 2017. www.bls.gov.
37. Lisa Bryan, "4 Steps to Health Coach Certification," Downshiftology, March 17, 2019. https://downshiftology.com.
38. International Sports Sciences Association, "The Qualities Found in a Good Nutrition Coach," 2019. www.issaonline.com.
39. Lisa Bryan, "5 Tips to a Successful Health Coaching Business," Downshiftology, March 6, 2018. https://downshiftology.com.

Fitness Instructor

40. Mallory Creveling, "7 Surprising Things I Learned About Teaching Group Fitness Classes When I Became an Instructor," *Self*, May 4, 2018. www.self.com.
41. Quoted in Natalie Morris "Date-Ercise Is the Speed Dating Fitness Class That Could Help You Find Love," Metro, July 25, 2019. https://metro.co.uk.
42. Quoted in American Council on Exercise, "What I've Learned as a Group Fitness Instructor," January 23, 2018. www.acefitness.org.
43. Quoted in American Council on Exercise, "What I've Learned as a Group Fitness Instructor."
44. Jessica Smith, "6 Things to Consider Before Becoming a Fitness Pro," *Shape*, 2019. www.shape.com.
45. Quoted in Smith, "6 Things to Consider Before Becoming a Fitness Pro."
46. Quoted in Smith, "6 Things to Consider Before Becoming a Fitness Pro."

Personal Trainer

47. Quoted in American Council on Exercise, "What I've Learned as a Group Fitness Instructor."
48. Quoted in Andy Orin, "Career Spotlight: What I Do as a Personal Trainer," Lifehacker, September 8, 2015. https://lifehacker.com.
49. National Federation of Professional Trainers, "The Role of a Personal Trainer," 2019. www.nfpt.com.
50. Quoted in Orin, "Career Spotlight."
51. Quoted in Smith, "6 Things to Consider Before Becoming a Fitness Pro."
52. Quoted in Orin, "Career Spotlight."

Interview with a Personal Trainer

Jan Gable is a self-employed personal trainer in San Diego, California. She started weight lifting at age fourteen and has experience in powerlifting, Olympic lifting, bodybuilding, and nutrition. In the 1980s Gable held the world record in four different weight classes in the bench press—the first women to do so at the time. Gable has worked as a personal trainer since 1986. She answered questions about her career as a personal trainer by email.

Q: Why did you become a personal trainer?
A: Having a degree in Health Science and being a powerlifter was a natural lead in for me to the occupation of Personal Training. When you train in a sport, say powerlifting or Olympic lifting, you learn the intricacies of that sport so you are better able to teach it to others.

Q: Can you describe your typical workday?
A: On a typical workday I'm up at 5 a.m. and off to the gym. I train four to six clients and then I take a break for one to two hours. After that I am back at the gym for one or two more clients. Mid-afternoon I do paperwork for my business and some networking. Following that, I'm back at the gym for two to four more training sessions.

Q: What do you like most about your job?
A: What I like most about my job is seeing the changes in my clients—not only physically, but also emotionally. When training clients, I use a process called Periodization. This program usually takes up to four months and starts with light weights and lots of reps. As the client progresses in the program, he or she gets

stronger as the weights increase and the reps drop to doubles or singles. This program emotionally challenges one's psyche. This process is repeated every four months and in so doing, the person will experience a continual increase in strength and internal fortitude. I find it very rewarding to see both the physical and emotional change in my clients!

Q: What do you like least about your job?
A: The thing I like least about my job is the schedule. Sometimes I work seven days a week—on and off sometimes 16 hours a day—with a varied schedule. This type of schedule is not too conducive for personal interests, taking classes or long vacations!

Q: What personal qualities do you find most valuable for this type of work?
A: Being passionate for learning all the different types of weightlifting—from the foundations of Olympic lifting and powerlifting, to the other modalities such as high intensity training (HIT), suspension training (TRX), and bodybuilding. And not only learning and experiencing all the different techniques of weightlifting, but being perceptive in interacting with your clients. This means truly LISTENING to the client. LISTENING might be the best quality for a personal trainer. Especially because sometimes someone is saying one thing but they really mean something else. Also, the quality of passion is important—a passion for learning. Keeping up on what is new and changing in your field is very key to being a good personal trainer.

Q: What is the best way to prepare for this type of job?
A: There are several steps to prepare for a career as a personal trainer:
> #1: Get an educational background in some type of science, for example, Physical Education, Kinesiology, or Health Science.
> #2: Get certified by a reputable coaching organization.

#3: Get CPR training.
#4: Get a business license.
#5: Get liability insurance.

Q: Why did you choose to be a self-employed trainer rather than be employed as a trainer at a company or gym?

A: I chose to be self-employed as a personal trainer because being self-employed you can choose your own hours. You also get to choose what interests you in regard to the specific direction you want to take as far as clientele; for example, working with aging populations or youth groups. Plus, you can work as much, or as little, as you want. By contrast, if you are employed by a facility or gym, you have to work the hours that are assigned to you. And you might not be able to choose the direction you might want to go as far as the type of clientele.

Q: What do you find challenging about being self-employed?

A: The most challenging things I find about being self-employed are having to find my own clients, and being on my own. If you're employed at a gym, you attend conferences and clinics together as a group. Plus you can share and teach each other what you have learned. This is not available to me as a self-employed personal trainer.

Q: What other advice do you have for students who might be interested in this career?

A: For those interested in a career as a personal trainer, there are four things I'd advise:

#1: Get certified by an organization that is reputable and has ongoing certification programs.

#2: Keep up your education in your chosen field.

#3: Expand your knowledge into other related areas such as yoga or Pilates, for example.

#4: Always be professional—both in attire and conduct!

Other Skilled Jobs in Wellness and Beauty

Barber
Beauty blogger/influencer
Beauty magazine editor
Beauty magazine writer
Beauty product designer
Bridal stylist
Celebrity beauty artist
Community health worker
Cosmetology school instructor
Cruise ship stylist
Dietitian
Editorial hairstylist
Eyelash technician
Fashion show stylist
Fitness coach
Gym owner
Hair color specialist
Hair extension/weave artist
Hairstylist
Hair technique educator
Health and wellness coordinator
Health coach
Health services manager

Health writer/blogger
Image consultant stylist
Laser hair removal specialist
Longevity wellness specialist
Makeup specialist
Meditation teacher
Perm specialist
Photo, TV, and movie stylist
Pilates instructor
Product manufacturer/inventor
Public health educator
Recreation program manager
Reiki healer
Running coach
Salon manager
Senior hair care specialist
Skin care specialist
Special effects makeup artist
Sports conditioning specialist
Theatrical or performance
   makeup artist
Weight loss coach
Zumba instructor

Editor's note: The online *Occupational Outlook Handbook* of the US Department of Labor's Bureau of Labor Statistics is an excellent source of information on jobs in hundreds of career fields, including many of those listed here. The *Occupational Outlook Handbook* may be accessed online at www.bls.gov/ooh.

Index